Remembering Sophia

A Valentinian Vespers for Gnostic Passersby

Ekka Nardo

First Edition

Copyright © 2020 by Ekka Nardo
γνῶστεία ἴδιος

Approved for use by the Rt. Reverend Stephan A. Hoeller, Regionary Bishop of the Ecclesia Gnostica. This vespers service may be used in addition to, or in lieu, of various vespers services for the Ecclesia Gnostica.

This service may be performed without the presence of the ordained clergy of the Ecclesia Gnostica.

October 2020

Approved by

✠ STEPHAN A. HOELLER
Regionary Bishop
Ecclesia Gnostica

Performance Details:

This work is designed to be read or to be performed as liturgy. As performance liturgy, it is flexibly designed for use by the solo practitioner or group, with or without the presence of Ecclesia Gnostica clergy. The liturgical format of this service uses a standard call (Celebrant) and response (All) for group use. Both cues would be read by a solo practitioner.

This service is brief and omits sections headings. The scriptural reading section is flexible. Use any appropriate text for personal services. See gnosis.org for quotable sources of gnostic literature.

Candles are optional. A quaternary array of candles can be used with a candle positioned at the 6, 9, 12, and 3 O'clock positions. If performing this service alone, the 6 O'clock candle is the one closest to the reader. If the service is celebrated or led by a prayer leader or clergy, the 6 O'clock candle is the one closest to the congregant audience.

Remembering Sophia

(If using the cardinal array of 4 candles, now light or begin with the 6 o'clock candle already lit. Adjust for audience.)

(C)   The LORD possessed me in the beginning of his way, before his works of old.

(C)   When there were no depths,
I was brought forth.
When he prepared the heavens,
I was there.
When he set a compass upon
the face of the deep, then
was I by him.

(A)   Hail Sophia, filled with light,
the Christ is with Thee,
blessed art Thou among the Aeons,
and blessed is the liberator of Thy light
Jesus.

(A)   Holy Sophia, Mother of all gods,
pray to the light for us thy children
now, and at the hour of our death.
Amen.

(Light 12, 9, 3 o'clock candles while reciting…)

(A) In the name of the Father, and the Son and the Holy Spirit. Amen.

(A) I shall seek that I may dwell in the house of the Lord all the days of my life

(P) The Lord said, "Fear not, for I have redeemed you; I have called you by name, you are mine."

(A) We are no more strangers and foreigners but fellow citizens with the Saints and the Household of God. And we are built upon a sure foundation, Christ himself being the Chief Corner Stone. In whom ye are also builded together to form an habitation of God through the Spirit. In whom the building fitly framed together groweth into a Holy Temple of the Lord. Except the Lord build the house: their labor is but lost that build it. The foundation of God standeth sure, having this seal: let everyone that nameth the name of Christ depart from iniquity. Christ is our Foundation and our Chief Corner Stone.

(A) O Lord, Thou hast created us to be immortal and made us to be an image of Thine own Eternity; yet often we forget the Glory of our Heritage and wander from the Path which leads to Righteousness. But Thou, O Lord, hast made us for Thyself and our hearts are ever restless till they find their rest in Thee. Look with the eyes of Thy Love upon our manifold imperfections and pardon all our shortcomings that we may be filled with the brightness of the Everlasting Light and become the unspotted mirror of Thy Power and the image of Thy Goodness; through Christ our Indwelling Lord. Amen.

(P) The Lord said, "I love those who love me; And those who diligently seek me will find me."

(A) The Spirit itself beareth witness with our spirit that we are the children of God.

(A) We invoke Thee, O Light of Lights, Who art above every power of the Father, Thou Who art called Light and Spirit and Life; for Thou hast reigned in our bodies for evermore. Amen.

(C) Jesus said, "Be as wise as serpents and as innocent as doves."

(A) Lord, place me where serpent meets dove that I might discern what to bear and what to set down.

(pause for reflection)

(P) The Light of the Cross binds all chaos.

(A) The light shines in the darkness, and the darkness has not overcome it.

(P) Reprove the wise and they will love you. Give instruction to the wise and they become wiser yet.

(P) (optional Gospel or scriptural reading, read as non-clergy or optional Munda Cor Meum when read by clergy)

(A) For this discernment and all your Divine Regard, I am grateful. I also give thanks to Thee for: …

(pause for reflection)

(A) As Sophia ever prays for us, so I here to now also pray, especially for those in need and mortal peril:

(pause for reflection)

(A) And for our beloved dead:

(pause for reflection)

(P) Jesus said, There is light within a man of light and it shines on the whole world. If they say to you, 'Where did you come from?', say to them:

(A) We came from the light.

(P) If they ask you, 'What is the sign of your father in you?', say to them,

(A) It is a movement and rest.

(A) Let the Light of the Divine Soul illumine us, that we may be guarded from distress and want: That all our days be perfect, holy and peaceful: that what is good and profitable for our souls and for the peace of the world may be granted us: that the rest of our lives may be spent in the knowledge of Truth. So let the Light of the Divine Soul illumine us. Amen.

(while extinguishing the 3 of 4 candles, leaving one lit)

(P) Jesus said, 'Become Passersby.'

The Quest for Gnostic Spirituality: You are Here.

The path to Gnostic spirituality winds through mysterious vales and haunted moors, so ascending to desolate peaks, where no human long abides. There are no tabernacles in these sacred places, for such ascents perennially renew themselves when the gnosis of one age becomes the shackles of another. Poems, love letters, and maps, the illuminated lacunae and visionary travelogues of the dead lay scattered in the katabatic catacombs of gnostic saints and monsters, bedazzled by the brazzled glean of tricksters – those holy hierophants who cover and reveal again the numinous ascent. Such maps, hardly won, are obscured again with the inked over, heavily imagined trails and the gerrymandered kingdoms of tyrants and history – the hierophant's last deception, the map itself, feignly surrendered, cruelly imposed.

Caveat emptor lest one spend the fortunes of life on a pearl that cannot be purchased. *Magic is work*.

The in-between wherein gnosis, gnostic, and gnosticism abide is a lawless swamp, the numinous vessel where demon and angel mingle. Dreams, visions, and nightmares –therein the penance paid with the unknotted myths, now those discordant strings of words – gnosis, gnostic, gnosticism. One flails. Thank God for words. From those bones and beating hearts of ancestors, words form again, inside out and in again, memories dream the past anew. To read is to resurrect the dead, to raise the God. *Reading is Magic*.

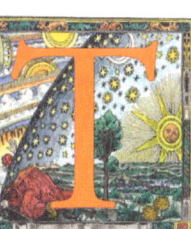

The lonely reader of these romantic words is thusly warned. Gnostic spirituality is not a philosophy, it is a practice, a discipline. Jesus said, "Split a piece of wood, and I am there. Lift up the stone, and you will find me there." The paradox of Gnostic spirituality: as we reach inward and upward, something reaches down to meet us in the small and big moments of life. This is why we must we must do more than think.

Prayer and reading are the practices available to the solitary practitioner of Gnostic spirituality. For some gnostics, prayer and participation in the sacramental *theurgia* is that practice or discipline. The global pandemic of 2020 sorely demonstrates what most practitioners of Gnostic spirituality already know — there is a lack of effective gnostic liturgy for those of us who cannot regularly attend gnostic churches or participate in gnostic communities. This prayer service is a pragmatic response to the reality that many of us cannot be present in a gnostic church to celebrate the Holy Gnostic Eucharist.

Vespers is an evening prayer service whose origin is found in the earliest days of the Christian church. Each major Christian tradition developed their own version of evening prayers. This Sophianic vespers service intends to provide Gnostic Christians with a spiritual practice that enhances one's overall sense of resiliency and spiritual appreciation. It can be privately read or privately performed.

Valentinian gnostics were also present in the early church, and they practiced the Sacraments and understood the salvific importance of Sophia, the hypostasized figure of Divine Feminine Wisdom. These myths tell us that Sophia is always near or present in humanity, ready to assist us. Wisdom reminds us of our familial home and leads us there if we are willing to be guided by Her. These myths and liturgies sustain us spiritually, especially when we are unable to participate in Eucharistic celebrations.

This work builds on the liturgical works of the Right Reverend Stephan A. Hoeller, the regionary bishop of the Ecclesia Gnostica. Hoeller was consecrated a bishop by Richard, Duc de Palatine in 1967 and established his church in the 1970's. This currently makes Hoeller the head of the longest standing neo-Gnostic Christian church (the Ecclesia Gnostica) in the United States. This liturgy is intended to *complement* Hoeller's Holy Gnostic Eucharist and

I leave it to the practitioner of these vespers to discern that for themselves.

Sojourners in gnostic realms quickly find they can quickly find gnostic texts "as-is" and without instructions or the benefit of tradition. Instantaneous access to information frequently results in instantaneous confusion. The minions of orthodoxy are ever ready to turn vision into dogma. More than ever, we need learned people, the gnostic hierophants who discern and resiliently affirm the Gnostic Mysteries in response to the continuing revelation of Eternal Gnosis. A carousel of keyhole views makes a mosaic of mystical texts that scintillates even as it frustrates one's attempts to work personal experience into praxis. Texts are contradictory and the older theories of gnosticism often have not responded to more recent discoveries of even older materials. The risk of traveling farther back into the history of the last 200 years of scholarship on gnosticism is that it moves us further away from the more recent scholarship dealing with even older gnostic sources that were not available until Hoeller's time. His engagement with those materials renewed and vindicated the best elements of less informed gnosticisms. Stephan Hoeller has filled this role as gnostic hierophant and lecturer for over 50 years now and one of his signature works on Gnosticism, *Gnosticism: New Light on the Ancient Tradition of Inner Knowing* is still the best starting place for the gnostic neophyte seeking to understand how Gnostic spirituality exists in American culture today.

Hoeller's liturgy and writings are a 20th century standard for gnostic spirituality because he reconciled Theosophical gnosticisms (pre-Nag Hammadi gnostic texts), Nag Hammadi gnostic texts, and the Depth Psychology of Carl Jung into a neo-gnostic Sacramental tradition. While all maps obscure the space they narrate, Hoeller's integrative works uniquely recognize the human being as the hermeneutic key that unlocks the Divine Self. Hoeller understood the various gnostic sources, both intellectually and spiritually, when he wrote his Gnostic Eucharist and Lectionary.

The harmony of Hoeller's gnostic *theoria* and

theurgia manifests in the poetic expression of his liturgy. This liturgy incorporates some of those elements (with permission) from Hoeller's Holy Gnostic Eucharist, Jewish Scripture (Old Testament), New Testament writings, Nag Hammadi texts, and Jungian thought. I am most grateful to Bishop Hoeller for his engagement with me on this work and his permission to use his materials. I hope you will agree that these are the rare imprimaturs of gnostic authenticity that make for compelling liturgy.

Feignly Surrendered: A Resource List

This material was introduced with a dire warning about the peril of intellectual maps. This was not to implant the idea that we can operate without them.

It is sufficient to acknowledge that we operate under the influence of one map or another. Take what works and leave the rest behind. To that end, as much as we seek to confirm or further our spiritual experiences, being open-minded to new ideas helps us build on old visions with new visions. When the vision is not renewed, the God Image dies.

This incomplete list of gnostic materials below draws on 3 main sources: Online writings by Stephan Hoeller from gnosis.org. Gnosis.org writings themselves – Lance Owens, a long-standing priest within the Ecclesia Gnostica, has built gnosis.org into an extensive repository of translated gnostic materials. While a subsection of gnosis.org is dedicated to the Ecclesia Gnostica, Owen's repository focuses on the direct presentation of texts. Hoeller's YouTube channel, Ecclesia Gnostica Clips is another source of both weekly homilies and his weekly lectures. The lectures here present a broad survey of Hoeller's lecture topics. The site is free and please subscribe and support the channel if you find it helpful.

The Ecclesia Gnostica currently has churches in Los Angeles, California; Portland, Oregon; and Austin, Texas. It is the oldest public gnostic sacramental tradition in the United States as of now. The Ecclesia Gnostica exists to uphold the Gnostic tradition and to administer the holy sacraments to those drawn to the altars of the Gnosis. The Regionary Bishop of the church, Stephan A. Hoeller, was consecrated to that office by the Duc de Palatine in 1967 and founded the Ecclesia Gnostica in 1970.

Use a QR app for your smart device to access the QR codes below.

 Hoeller's *Gnosticism: New Light on the Ancient Tradition of Inner Knowing.*

 Bishop Hoeller's YouTube homily and lecture channel. An extensive set of Sunday lectures and Friday night Gnostic Society Lectures. Also, check here for online, live performances of these vespers.

 What is a Gnostic?

 The Gnostic Worldview

Secret Sayings of Jesus

The Gnostic Mythic Pattern of the Journey of the Soul:

Right Reverend, Steven Marshall, Auxiliary Bishop, regular online services and an excellent newsletter.
http://gnosticchurchportland.org/

April D. Deconick, Bruzauskas & Hauschildt professionally narrate and perform initiatic readings of Nag Hammadi texts.

Image Credits:

Book Cover: www.iStockphoto.com "Fire Dancer at Night" by myshkovsky, id 480698484, id 480698482

Cellarius, Andreas.. "Planisphaerium Ptolemaicum siue machina orbium mundi ex hypothesi Ptolemaica in plano disposita." Map. 1661. Map reproduction courtesy of the Norman B. Leventhal Map & Education Center at the Boston Public Library"

Flammarion Engraving from Flammarion's 1888 L'atmosphère : météorologie popu-laire

0mela # 22907575 VectorStock.com, licensed
vtorous # 13269429 VectorStock.com, licensed.

www.ingramcontent.com/pod-product-compliance
Lightning Source LLC
Chambersburg PA
CBHW042235090526
44589CB00001B/11